HAL LEONARD UKULELE FOR KIDS SONGBOOK

UKULELE METHOD

AUDIO ACCESS INCLUDED

Strum the Chords Along with 10 Popular Songs

T0039720

PLAYBACK+
Speed • Pitch • Balance • Loop

ISBN 978-1-4950-5117-3

7777 W. BLUEMOUND RD. P.O. BOX 13819 MILWAUKEE, WI 53213

Visit Hal Leonard Online at
www.halleonard.com

THE SIAMESE CAT SONG
from Walt Disney's LADY AND THE TRAMP

Words and Music by Peggy Lee
and Sonny Burke

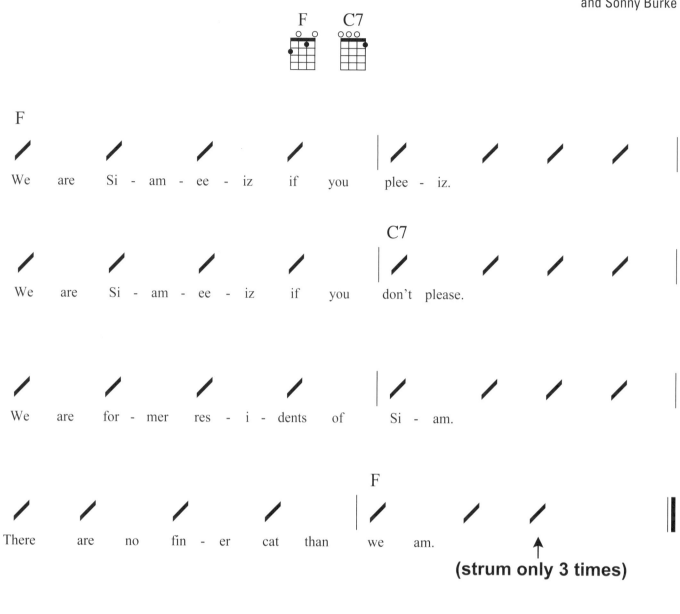

We are Si - am - ee - iz if you plee - iz.

We are Si - am - ee - iz if you don't please.

We are for - mer res - i - dents of Si - am.

There are no fin - er cat than we am.

(strum only 3 times)

TEACHER MELODY:

SUPERCALIFRAGILISTICEXPIALIDOCIOUS

from Walt Disney's MARY POPPINS

Words and Music by Richard M. Sherman
and Robert B. Sherman

TEACHER MELODY:

RIPTIDE

Words and Music by
Vance Joy

Am   G   C

Am ... **G** ... **C**

La - dy, running down to the rip - tide, taken away to the

Am ... **G** ... **C**

dark side, I wanna be your left - hand man. I

Am ... **G** ... **C**

love you when you're sing - ing that song, and I got a lump in my

Am ... **G** ... **C**

throat 'cause you're gonna sing the words wrong.

(strum only 3 times)

TEACHER MELODY:

This page is intentionally left blank to avoid an unnecessary page turn.

I STILL HAVEN'T FOUND WHAT I'M LOOKING FOR

Words and Music by
U2

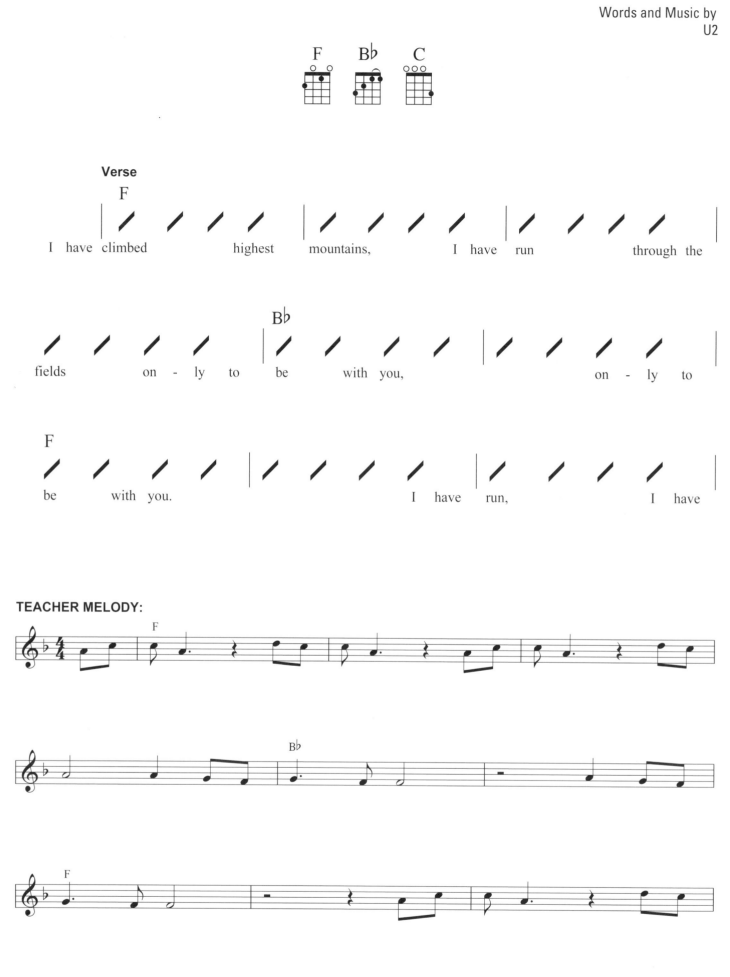

Verse

F

I have climbed highest mountains, I have run through the

Bb

fields on - ly to be with you, on - ly to

F

be with you. I have run, I have

TEACHER MELODY:

UP AROUND THE BEND

Words and Music by
John Fogerty

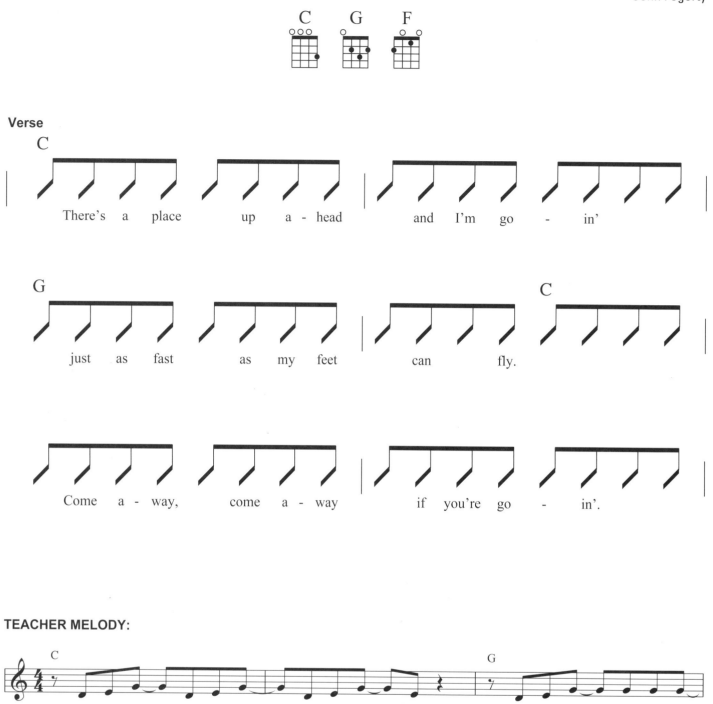

Verse

There's a place up a-head and I'm go - in'

just as fast as my feet can fly.

Come a - way, come a - way if you're go - in'.

TEACHER MELODY:

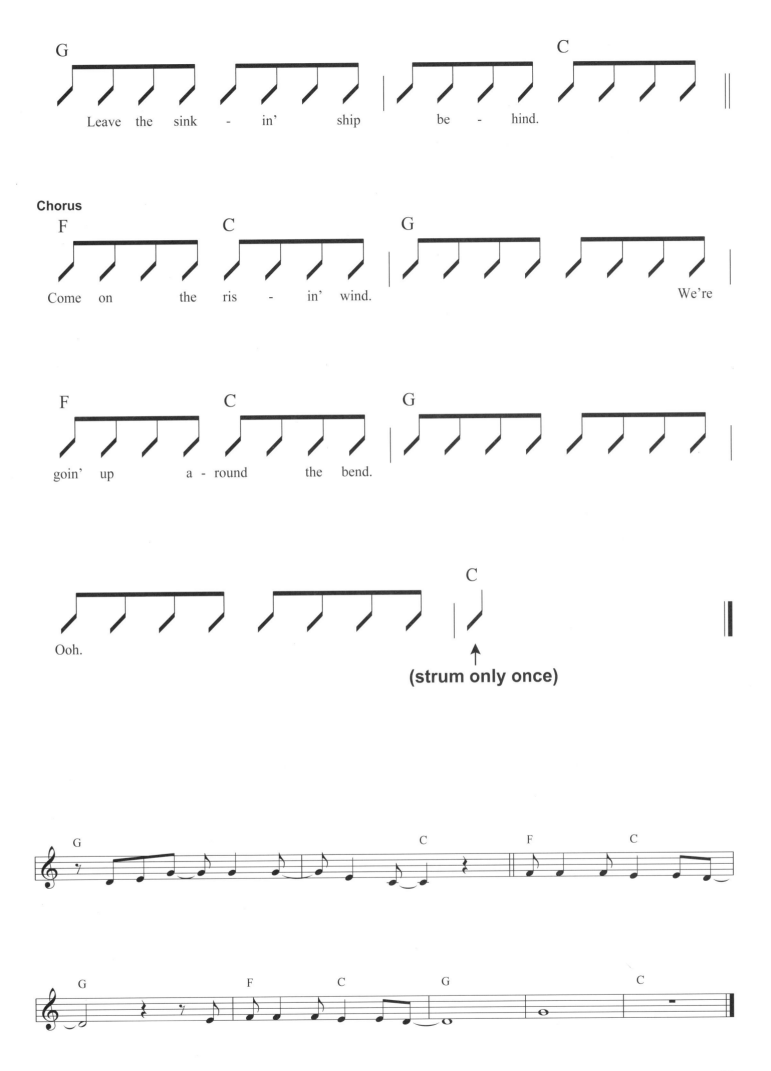

Leave the sink - in' ship be - hind.

Chorus

Come on the ris - in' wind.

We're goin' up a - round the bend.

Ooh.

(strum only once)

This page is intentionally left blank to avoid an unnecessary page turn.

HOW MUCH IS THAT DOGGIE IN THE WINDOW

Words and Music by
Bob Merrill

TEACHER MELODY:

THE LION SLEEPS TONIGHT

New Lyrics and Revised Music by
George David Weiss, Hugo Peretti
and Luigi Creatore

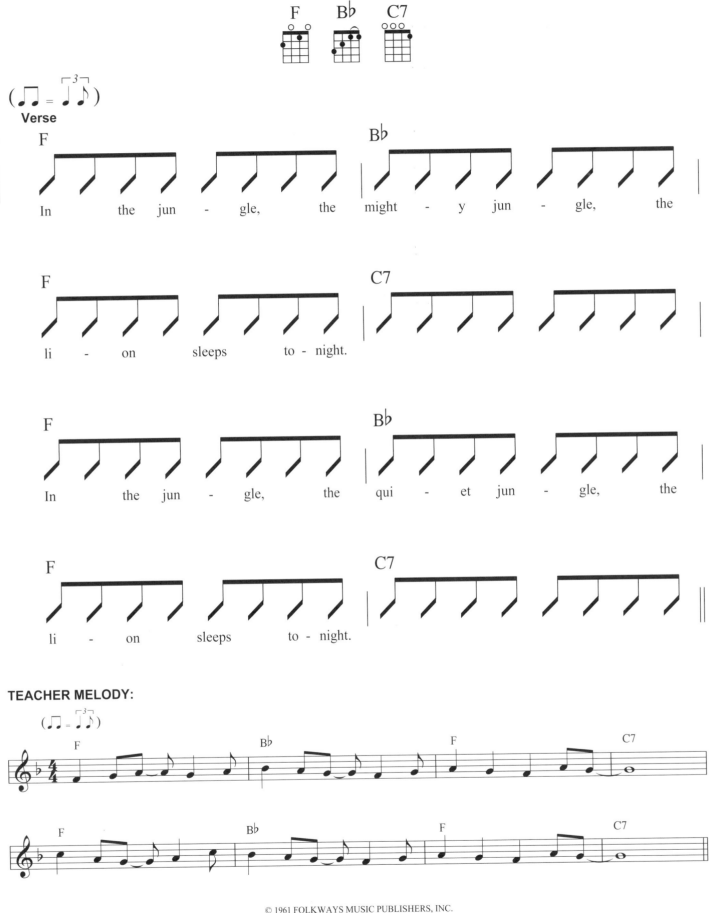

Verse

In the jun - gle, the might - y jun - gle, the
li - on sleeps to - night.
In the jun - gle, the qui - et jun - gle, the
li - on sleeps to - night.

TEACHER MELODY:

Chorus

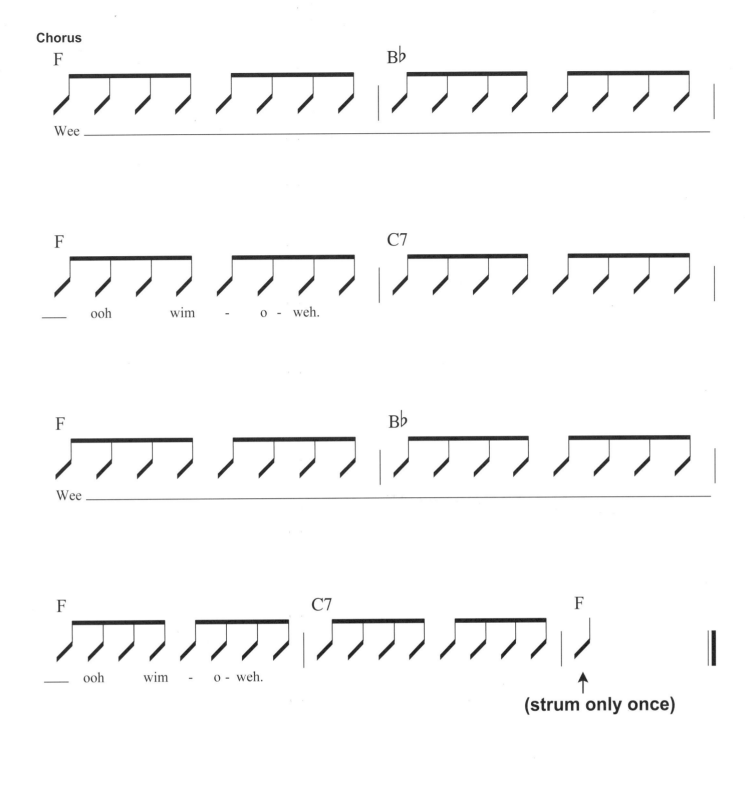

(strum only once)

DON'T WORRY, BE HAPPY

Words and Music by
Bobby McFerrin

Verse

F

Here's a lit - tle song I wrote. You

Gm   B♭

might want to sing it note for note. Don't wor - ry,

F   B♭   F   B♭

be hap - py.

F

In ev - 'ry life we have some trou - ble,

TEACHER MELODY:

Gm
but when you wor - ry you make

it dou - ble. Don't

B♭
wor - ry,

F **B♭**
be hap - py. *Don't*

F **B♭** **Chorus** **F**
wor - ry, be hap - py. Ooh. _____

Gm **B♭**
_____ Ooh. _____

F **B♭** **F** **B♭** **F**
Ooh. _____

(strum only once)

STAND BY ME

Words and Music by Jerry Leiber,
Mike Stoller and Ben E. King

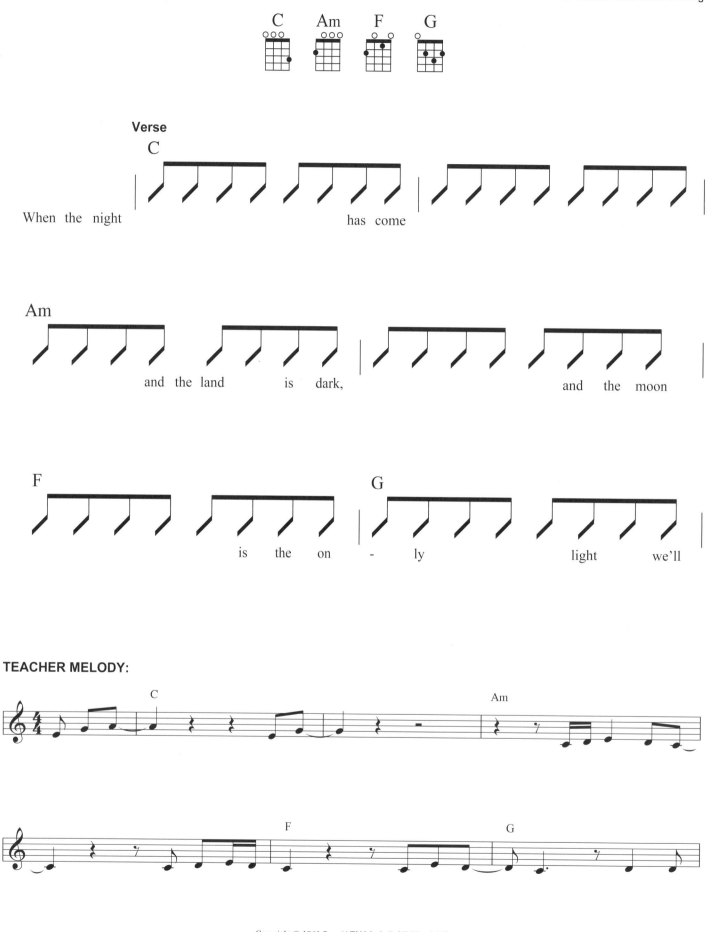

TEACHER MELODY:

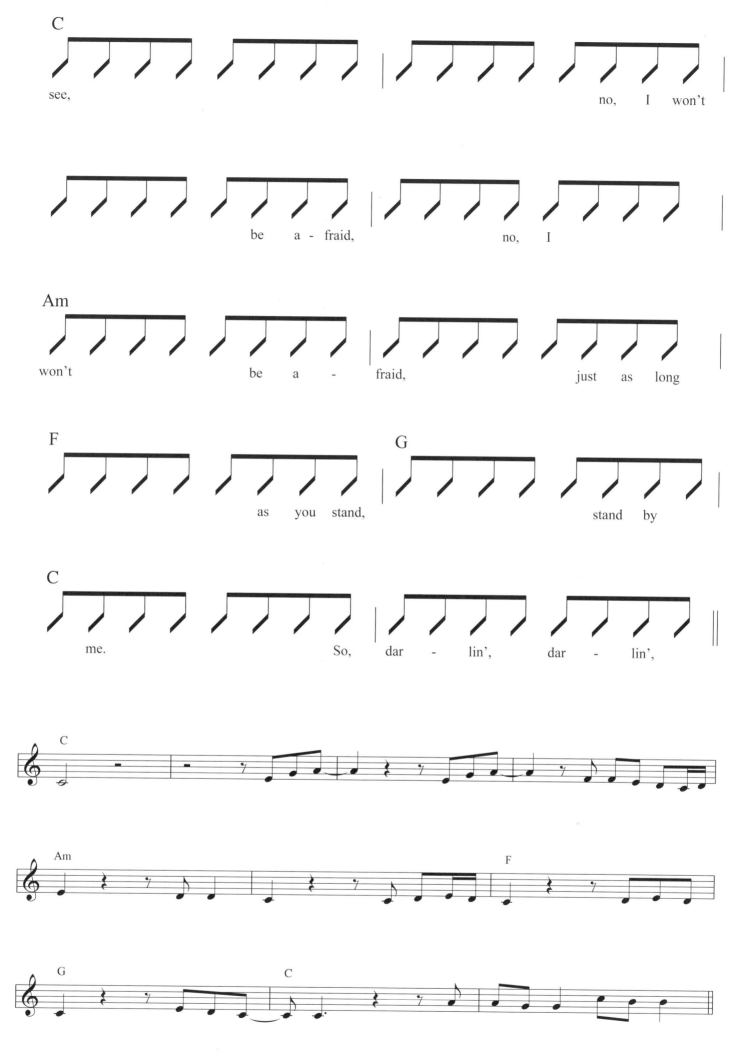

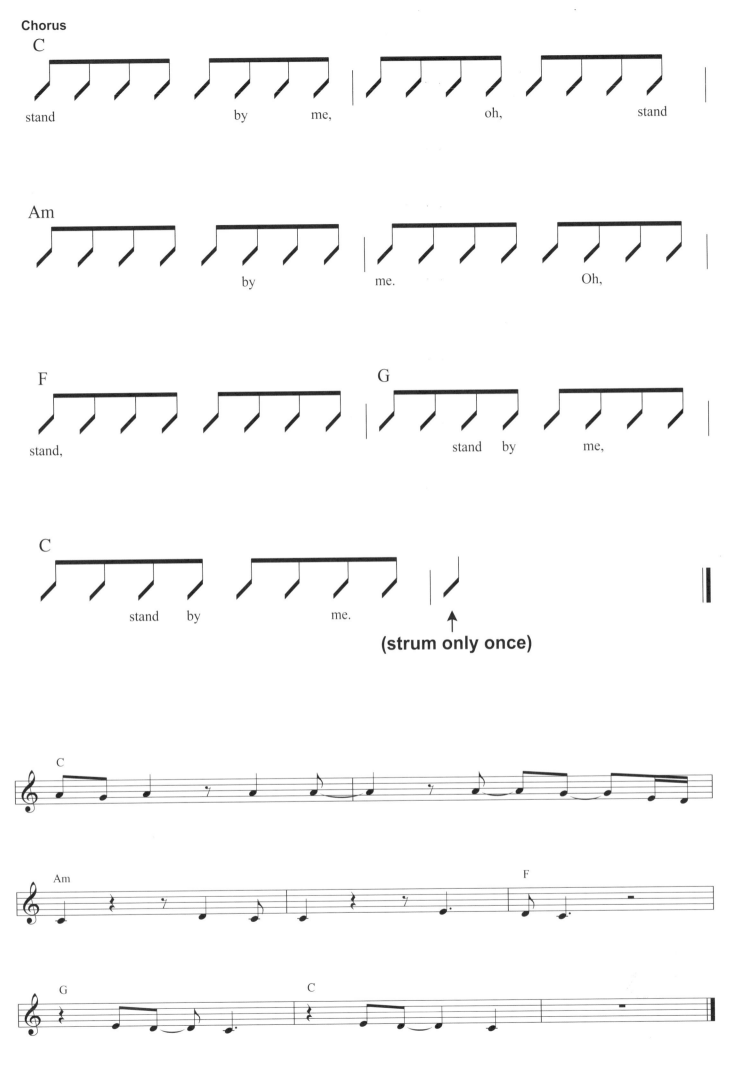

I'M YOURS

Words and Music by
Jason Mraz

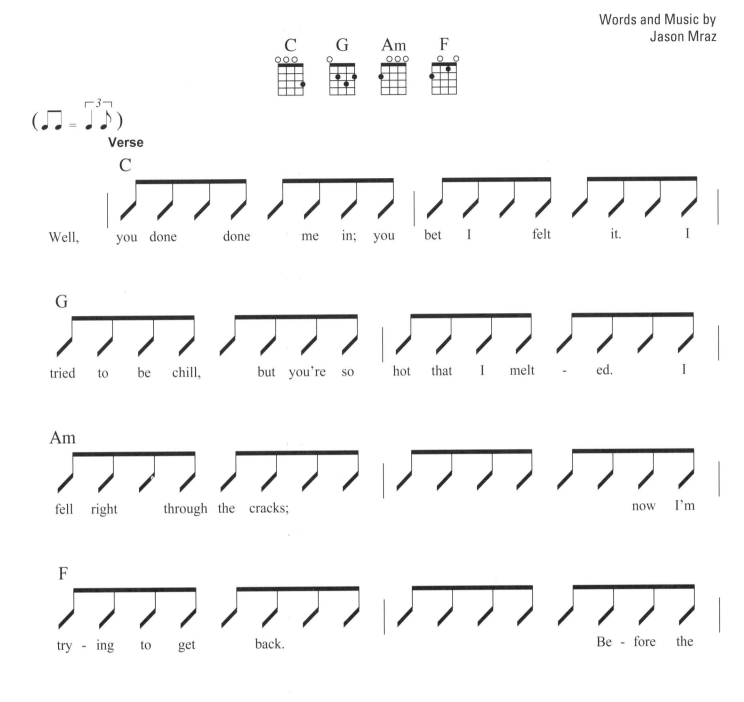

TEACHER MELODY:

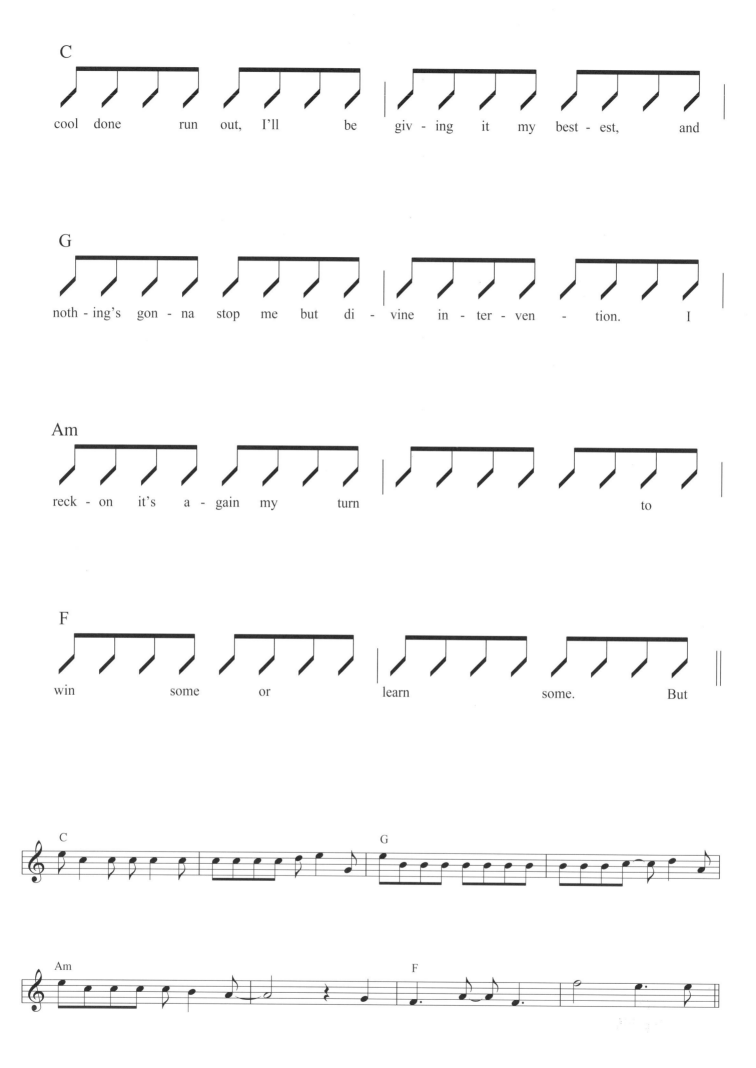

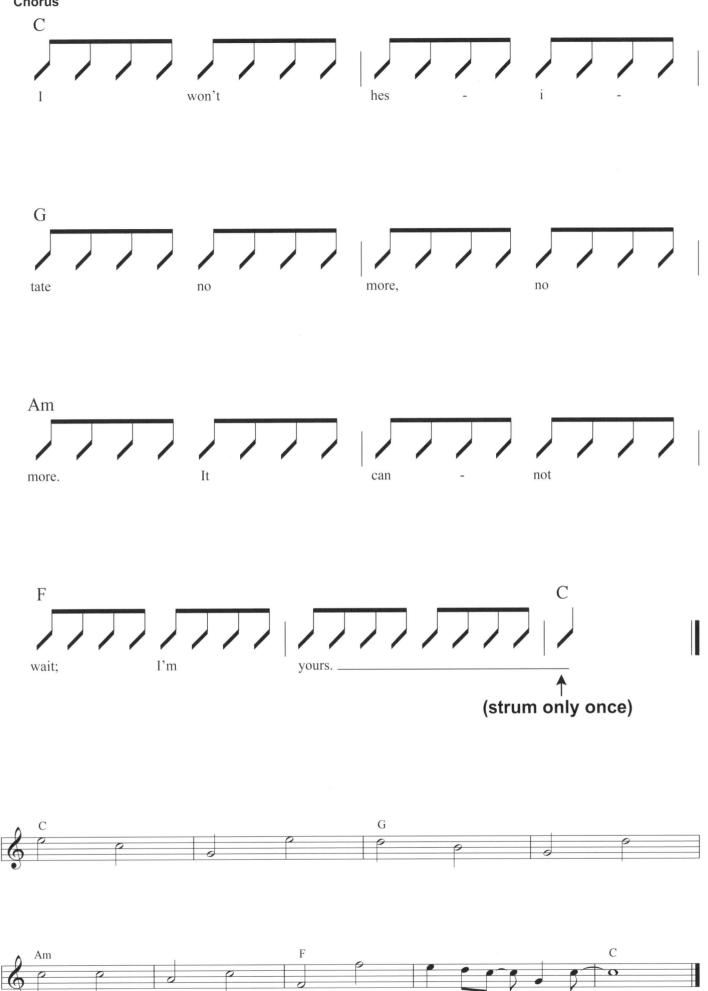

UKULELE CHORD SONGBOOKS

This series features convenient 6" x 9" books with complete lyrics and chord symbols for dozens of great songs. Each song also includes chord grids at the top of every page and the first notes of the melody for easy reference.

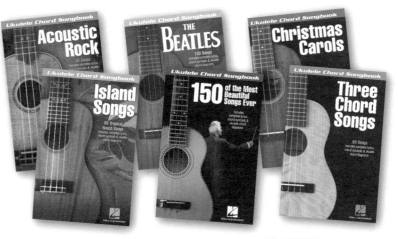

ACOUSTIC ROCK

60 tunes: American Pie • Band on the Run • Catch the Wind • Daydream • Every Rose Has Its Thorn • Hallelujah • Iris • More Than Words • Patience • The Sound of Silence • Space Oddity • Sweet Talkin' Woman • Wake up Little Susie • Who'll Stop the Rain • and more.
00702482 . . . . $15.99

THE BEATLES

100 favorites: Across the Universe • Carry That Weight • Dear Prudence • Good Day Sunshine • Here Comes the Sun • If I Fell • Love Me Do • Michelle • Ob-La-Di, Ob-La-Da • Revolution • Something • Ticket to Ride • We Can Work It Out • and many more.
00703065 . . . . $19.99

BEST SONGS EVER

70 songs: All I Ask of You • Bewitched • Edelweiss • Just the Way You Are • Let It Be • Memory • Moon River • Over the Rainbow • Someone to Watch over Me • Unchained Melody • You Are the Sunshine of My Life • You Raise Me Up • and more.
00117050 . . . . $16.99

CHILDREN'S SONGS

80 classics: Alphabet Song • "C" Is for Cookie • Do-Re-Mi • I'm Popeye the Sailor Man • Mickey Mouse March • Oh! Susanna • Polly Wolly Doodle • Puff the Magic Dragon • The Rainbow Connection • Sing • Three Little Fishies (Itty Bitty Poo) • and many more.
00702473 . . . . $14.99

CHRISTMAS CAROLS

75 favorites: Away in a Manger • Coventry Carol • The First Noel • Good King Wenceslas • Hark! the Herald Angels Sing • I Saw Three Ships • Joy to the World • O Little Town of Bethlehem • Still, Still, Still • Up on the Housetop • What Child Is This? • and more.
00702474 . . . . $14.99

CHRISTMAS SONGS

55 Christmas classics: Do They Know It's Christmas? • Frosty the Snow Man • Happy Xmas (War Is Over) • Jingle-Bell Rock • Little Saint Nick • The Most Wonderful Time of the Year • White Christmas • and more.
00101776 . . . . $14.99

ISLAND SONGS

60 beach party tunes: Blue Hawaii • Day-O (The Banana Boat Song) • Don't Worry, Be Happy • Island Girl • Kokomo • Lovely Hula Girl • Mele Kalikimaka • Red, Red Wine • Surfer Girl • Tiny Bubbles • Ukulele Lady • and many more.
00702471 . . . . $16.99

150 OF THE MOST BEAUTIFUL SONGS EVER

150 melodies: Always • Bewitched • Candle in the Wind • Endless Love • In the Still of the Night • Just the Way You Are • Memory • The Nearness of You • People • The Rainbow Connection • Smile • Unchained Melody • What a Wonderful World • Yesterday • and more.
00117051 . . . . $24.99

PETER, PAUL & MARY

Over 40 songs: And When I Die • Blowin' in the Wind • Goodnight, Irene • If I Had a Hammer (The Hammer Song) • Leaving on a Jet Plane • Puff the Magic Dragon • This Land Is Your Land • We Shall Overcome • Where Have All the Flowers Gone? • and more.
00121822 . . . . $12.99

THREE CHORD SONGS

60 songs: Bad Case of Loving You • Bang a Gong (Get It On) • Blue Suede Shoes • Cecilia • Get Back • Hound Dog • Kiss • Me and Bobby McGee • Not Fade Away • Rock This Town • Sweet Home Chicago • Twist and Shout • You Are My Sunshine • and more.
00702483 . . . . $14.99

TOP HITS

31 hits: The A Team • Born This Way • Forget You • Ho Hey • Jar of Hearts • Little Talks • Need You Now • Rolling in the Deep • Teenage Dream • Titanium • We Are Never Ever Getting Back Together • and more.
00115929 . . . . $14.99

Prices, contents, and availability subject to change without notice.

HAL•LEONARD®

www.halleonard.com

0818
238